Welcome to
the Grand Hotel

By the same author

Points of Contact (1963)
A Long Time Burning (1969)
Treason and Libel: State Trials, vol. 1 (1972)
The Public Conscience: State Trials, vol. 2 (1972)
Prince Charlie's Bluff (1974)
Charge! Hurrah! Hurrah! (1974)

Welcome to
the Grand Hotel

Donald Thomas

LONDON AND BOSTON

Routledge & Kegan Paul

First published in 1975
by Routledge & Kegan Paul Ltd
Broadway House, 68–74 Carter Lane
London EC4V 5EL and
9 Park Street, Boston, Mass. 02108, USA
Set in Monotype Bembo
and printed in Great Britain by
Ebenezer Baylis & Son Limited
The Trinity Press, Worcester, and London
ISBN 0 7100 8104 9

Contents

Acknowledgments

Acknowledgments are due to the BBC programmes 'The Poet's Voice', 'Poetry Now' and 'New Poetry', as well as to the following publications, in which a number of these poems have appeared: *Critical Quarterly, Kenyon Review, Listener, New Statesman, Quarterly Review of Literature* and *Spectator*.

Loss is their shadow-wife. Anxiety
Receives them like a grand hotel.

W. H. Auden, *In Time of War*

I

Ensign Carruthers

Hours in a Library

Identitas.
Carruthers kept back-numbers
Of *Transactions of the Bibliographical Society*,
The one professed umbilical that wound into his past.

An open man, Carruthers, mostly. All his shelves were kept on
    view
But for one cupboard. And what's there?
Carruthers' wife and grown-up sons know locks
Will not be opened by a loving look.

Often you must have wondered what he kept there,
(As most did)
Behind the panelled oak and double lock.
A brothel for old books was how most people saw it,
And so for each the secret horde
Mirrored a life's ambition.
Memoirs of some Renaissance pederast;
Complete De Sade, or sagas of the lash;
Second Empire novels, lilac tints on black,
Smooth as a thigh, responsive as a lip.
O, *Cercle du Livre Précieux!*
O, *Bibliothèque des Curieux!*

Men
(Women too)
Hoped.
Found Carruthers irresistible at parties. Hoped
For news of something unimaginable.

One day, drinking at his place, found a key.
Someone unlocked. Nails clawed. Snatched books. Eyes read.

'At the end of term, the House lost three School Prefects:
   Curll, E., Wilkes, J., and Carruthers, R. P.'

Read *Headmaster's Notes.*
'Learning to help the not-so-likeable chap is a lesson we might
   all profit by.'

Read.
' " Don't worry, you fellows," said Ratty, "We'll catch the
   bounders after lock-up." '

Read.
'After torrential rain in the first weeks of term, the 1st XV
   surrendered the rugger-pitch to the ducks.'

No one invites Carruthers anywhere now,
Not now we know his abnormality
(Though in some ways, now the shock's over, you can't help
   laughing)
Is infinitely worse and more embarrassing than anyone could
   have imagined.
Inevitably, one still meets him at work,
Though, knowing what one does, it's awfully hard to find
   anything to say.
We all felt that the incident taught us a lesson, anyhow.

Oh, never do what poor Carruthers did.
Oh, never leave *your* cupboard key around.

Curriculum Vitæ

Master Carruthers' treat at six years old,
Better, said Granny, than the barred tigers
Or chained ape—than summer floss or hot sand's gold.
A goddess held him. Gas sang in his ears.
Eyes woke in the blood's bright city
Of Tonsilectomy.

Proconsul of an adolescent tribe,
Carruthers' beauty and his sleight of hand
Turned sport to art. At eighteen saved the match,
Stopping a ball full in his winning smile
To earn House Colours and a plate of teeth.

Outfitted for the greater game of life,
Ensign Carruthers led to bridal bed
By none less than his Colonel's daughter, found
His fortune unbelievable. But all his sleight
Of hand would never save this match.
Mrs Carruthers left to do what's right
By an invalid aunt of six-foot-two
With a green Mercedes and Guards' moustache.
Deprived Carruthers moped, and read
Count Fanny's Nuptials by his empty grate.

Among the fives cups and the 1st XVs
In sepia on his walls, the ambience of Apollo
Lingered on. In middle age, the hostile sneers
Described Carruthers (fat by thirty-five)
As 'still replete with promise unfulfilled.'

After the first real fright, he saw his blood
Sparkle on white enamel. The doctor smiled

And reassured. A touch of nothing much
To cause concern. But while he hemmed,
In his stage-prompter's cough, to still all doubts,
The mutes and weepers with their black crape veils
Shuffled impatiently upon the stairs.

The Next One

Like angels ever bright and fair
The crossed blades lisp above his hair,
Locked by the screw's steel knuckle while they cut
An arabesque from air.
The black, pneumatic throne revolves
To every angle of the day,
While bay-rum scents and scalp-massage
Encapsulate this morning hour.

'Mr Carruthers, please.'
The surgeon-barber smiles.
Carruthers in his borrowed grace
Fidgets, detects the unseen skin that flakes and scales
As cut flock, greyer now, skims the tiled floor.

At his left hand a houri sits and trims
His splintered cuticle. The lower stool
On which her spread rump fills her overall
To pink balloon, confirms his altitude.
Head bent, submissive, glancing at his words,
Her phrases, like a yashmak, still reveal
Her plucked eyes' tedium.

Carruthers counts her like a pile
Of small coin. Paint or not,
A face you'd change with fifty such
And never know the odds.

The angel scissors sing
How sweet disease and death shall raise
Even Carruthers to equality
With satin thighs and new-born love.
Celeste and dulcimer discourse
Their rival themes and lock at last:

2

'I never buy in bulk except
I get a discount that I really like. . . .'
'. . . You can't afford embarrassments,
Like having stock hang on and on.'

Lacquer of steel on silk, the girl's bowed head
Fixes his gaze. Drowsy from the massage,
He guesses at the blemishes
Under her skin of clothes.
She may yet die, the makeshift stitching burst,
At twenty-five.
Carruthers, passionless, shall live
A second fifty years, now undisturbed
Even by Grecian youth in flannel suits.

And, soon or late, she'll come to this,
The favour of the waiting-room,
And dread the angel of the knife
Whose harbinger stands tall and smart,
(His Aphrodite in a buttoned coat)
Smiling false reassurance with her words,
'Mr Carruthers, please.'

Parque de Maria Luisa

Moonlight.
Black evergreen in underworlds.
Pathos among night cypresses
Makes him the mark for each petitioner
Among his fading dead, who loiter tile by tile
Along the blue ceramic path,
Begging remembrance awhile
With wooden bowls.
His Baedeker falls open where the ribbon marked.
'Rewards to mendicants,' the book of life insists,
'Are rarely in their own best interests.
Notice, however, where the German band
Plays favourites from light opera at dusk.'

In Venusberg there grows a tree
Whose lanterns glow like blood:
In Venusberg the shade falls red
And wine-light flows. . . .

Over each cup and ghost of steam,
Tall girls inhale Brazil and dream.
Words ring like coin on the iron tables,
Knees open other knees,
A letter from the dead engages him.

'Well done, my boy! Alive at fifty-three!
Admit, at ten, you never thought you'd be.
But "writing on the wall", as you now realise,
Is only someone's tender for a pair of thighs
When any race, creed, caste, or sex will do.
You'll find your way around the menu too,
Beauty deserts you but not acumen.
(Discrimination just means knowing when
To send back pâté to the chef

But take whatever girl the rest have left.)
Forget the envious years you lived on scraps
While buttocks like cleft plums fell in your lap.
A fool could tell you this—but still I'd rather.
Adieu! Posthumously, your natural father.'

Carruthers rose to go.

'P.S. Does it still warm you like a cloak,
Your inability to see the joke?'

Pompe Funebre

A clash of symbols. In a plush cortège
Carruthers passes to his marble tomb
(An obelisk in strawberry-pink).

While tropic seas, clear apple-green,
Sigh to the sparkling promenade,
A negress sheathed in ponyskin
Reins the black horses of the windowed hearse.
Her body moves and lingers
In the changing attitudes Carruthers loved.
To tossing plume the salon music calls
And bland crescendos of a Chopin waltz
Oil the wheels of afternoon.

Then to the tree-lined boulevards.
His loyal dwarfs,
His mutes with brass and drum,
Draw sobs from *Tannhäuser*, the overture.
The crowd falls still: the hero passes by.
From each lamp's flower-basket weeps
A scarf in black chiffon.

Black, too, the stockings of a dozen girls
Who, naked otherwise (the way he liked them),
Posture as weepers round the hearse.
Perfume of dying flowers, a rich decay,
Where blown hair twines with wreaths,
And each tall goddess bulges

Breasts, rump, thighs, pudenda,
As her late belovèd chose,
For this *grande messe des morts*.
From the kerb, their younger sisters watch and smile,
Sly tongues exploring ice-cream cones,

And sleek with sun-tan oil beneath their veils.
Temples of *haute couture* display each fetish
Upon a living model (in his honour):
Booted and furred, foot on a neck,
Or bowed with chains: the ways he liked.

But round the final corner all was real again:
Carruthers, plus two undertaker's men,
Plus three acquaintances. A taxi-load,
Who came to see him burn.

The glass-walled chapel disavowed
All thimble-rigging.
While an official prayer was read,
The mourners watched the summer world outside.

A woman in a garden cuffed her child.
Embossed upon the pale back of her thighs,
A lavatory seat, like a pink brand,
Ran between sunsuit and fat knees.
Flesh dimpling on slack muscle at each step
Winked back the world's farewell to Tannhäuser.

Soft electronic harps took up
A programmed descant. The flame burned white.
And when he heard his own hair catch,
Carruthers woke, and died of fright.

2

Welcome to the Grand Hotel

The Countryside in June

The tiny creatures smacked and spat
In a paste of their blood on the perspex shield.
Hedgehog and rabbit, pressed to a flat pelt,
Quilted the asphalt where the tyre scuffed grit.
Their knees touched, curving the last long bend,
While the engine raced at a deep snarl
And took the hill cleanly. The polished car
Idled to silence by the next field.

The goose-grass wound too feebly round their legs
Its sticky tape. Thistles tore shins. The coarse sting
Of nettles lanced her nylons, burning
Smooth legs in acid with a barbed caress.
Brambles round hedge emplacements brought him down,
Like a man caught on the wire. The sudden burrows
Lay like a minefield to fell him. Pale boughs
Of saplings recoiled in a whip's thong.

Methodically, he beat the thorns,
Left the young trees maimed, their sap bleeding,
To make the place safe for her. Then, turning
A little dial, he drowned the birds' thin song.

On their picnic bed he reached out to her,
Handing her chocolates that she squirmed in choosing,
But laid the softest in her mouth, without seeing
The wasp, which had hardly seen her either.

In the watering mouth her little teeth met, closing
Straight through the neck. The severed brain
Willed the tail's reflex to pump the sting
Into her tongue, with a Borgeian cunning.

Back to the car he dragged her, the tongue
Bulging, a fleshy gag in her throat,
Then drove like Jehu, while his darling choked,
For whom the shortest road was all too long.

The Audience is Leaving

The audience is leaving,
Though in their yellow shoal
Of light that glows like wax
The string quartet still threads
A counterpoint of charm.

In the lit park how air lingers
Like exhalations of smoke
In the perfumed oxygen of night.
A jacaranda tree in flower
Blooms with a skull
That winter rain whitened.

The audience is leaving,
Not caring that Mozart's *andante*
'States extremes of mood,
Often throwing into prominence
The lower staves.'

The 'cellist, too, allows
His mind its liberty,
Catching the oval pallor
And her hair's dark sweep
Of a girl in the front row,
Feeling her bare thighs clasp his neck.
He dreams of Mozart still
But lives for this.

The audience is leaving:
Not from the back rows alone
But from the front as well
They clutch their coats and go.

The viola is silent.
The 'cellist, limping from the stage,
Retires, puts on
A new moustache,
And heads for the lights among the trees.

The audience is leaving:
In duet, the violins alone
Play to the empty chairs,
Until the resolution of the themes
Obliges them to rise, bow,
Smile expansively, and go.

Before a crowd of hundreds in the park,
The 'cellist swings an axe
And at the first gash
Draws a gush of blood
From the jacaranda tree.

The audience has left:
Tables are swept and the park unlit.
But the night grows warmer
While footfalls of leopard and cat
By deadened trails
Converge on the temple
In its derelict moonlight.

Children's Game

How would you like to be executed,
Supposing you had to be executed?

'Oh, I don't know,' said Samways, sharpening sticks,
After his birthday tea—eleven years old,
'I think I'd pick being shot. It's fast, at least.'

'And what,' said Kendrick, 'if they missed,
And got you in the guts? Only one rifle's loaded.
All the rest have blanks, so no one knows who did it.
Just suppose his hand shook when he fired.
You'd have to wait for quite a while.
I'd have my head off—guillotined.'

'Except you'd hear it coming down,' said Gosse.
'How about something like they do in books?
They lock you in a cage and let you drop
Into a river. Then they watch
The water rising. All the time
You're trying to press your face towards the roof.'

'Enough of that,' said gentle Mr Stokes,
Too old to be conscripted for the war,
'Time you were all asleep, not chattering
Such nonsense.' Silence. And the light went out.

It wasn't nonsense in the years to come.
Pneumonia, in his coma, came to Gosse,
Filling the space his ribs caged
With alluvial slime no river bed
Could rival. In the dark
He pressed for the roof in vain.

A windshield edge sheared Kendrick at the neck,
Cleanly as any headsman might have done.
And what got Samways, in its way,
Was powerful as a dum-dum fired low,
But lasting many times as long.
Morphia, like a blindfold, kept him calm,
Muffling the knowledge that it might be months
Before the provost-marshal would reload.

The Blue Train

Light-codes beat on the blinds
In the night from the Blue Train:
Tunnels roar through sleep
Where the Blue Train goes.

There is room for all on the Blue Train,
THE BLUE TRAIN, the blue train:
There are no complaints on the Blue Train,
And the Blue Train never stops. . . .

It is reliably reported from the Restaurant Car that Count
Significance has solved the problem of making the final bottle
of Château d'Yquem last for ever, by pouring each glassful half
the size of the one before.

The drink is free on the Blue Train,
THE BLUE TRAIN, the blue train:
Nobody pays on the Blue Train,
And no one ever owes.

Inches away, a tunnel wall smashes by at 90. The night-cold
rushes like a hill stream against the smooth flanks of the steel
coachwork. Hermetic blinds seal carriage windows against the
plains of moonlight. The Sleeping Car attendant hardly hears the
voices of the medical team as they sit on bunk edges, backs to
polished walnut, and watch Susie and Sally fight naked on the
travelling carpet among scents of Chanel and scattered Eau de
Nil, and mud supplied on request. The Captain tears silk; mascara
dribbles; he pats a pale thigh as it fences against a protagonist's
arm, 'Fight, you two, it's what you're here for.' No one breathes.
There is curtain of hair torn and nails, there is. . . .

> Blood being served in the buffet
> With steak, on the Blue Train.
> You can eat what you like on the Blue Train
> And always like what you eat.

At the quiet end of the Wagon Lit, Belinda puts on her black velvet collar, bangles of copper, and rings of gold. Naked otherwise, she takes a deep breath and arranges herself on the cold leather like a goose, waiting for Lord Finger. He, however, is in the Smoking Car, where he has just trumped Sir Luck's ace with a Smith & Wesson ·38.

> If you want a girl on the Blue Train,
> Or a boy or both on the Blue Train,
> You should sit where you are on the Blue Train
> And ring for love's reward.

Whatever it was he did to Belinda, the wretched girl died of it. His Lordship rages at the attendant, demanding SATISFACTION. A replacement is chosen at last. Lord Finger smiles and all ends amicably. But, 'The snake with its tail in its mouth is an emblem of self-consuming desire,' says the attendant sadly, indicating the engine of the Blue Train which is rapidly gaining upon the guard's van.

> When a train keeps time like a secret,
> It's the Blue Train, the Blue Train:
> The Blue Train runs on time
> As other wheels do on rails.
> There is room for all on the Blue Train,
> THE BLUE TRAIN, the blue train:
> The Blue Train is just leaving,
> Anywhere.

Welcome to the Grand Hotel

Jawbone shot loose, the dying leopard ran
With killer teeth hung in a slack grimace.
Cleaned now, that tawny pelt beds her lank thighs.
A python's tube of skin, cut for her shoes,
Taken so fast the leer of venomed head
Still threshed, although the blade had gutted him.

She knew that frightened animals grow tense
But death in these kitchens sealed soft flavours in
By pan and knife, like sterile surgery.
It spoilt the texture if a lobster died
Of scalding, not of gradual heat-exhaustion.
Man's exercise of privilege is taste.

Dressed for the afternoon with chiffon trails
Of scarves and veils, she breathed the glittering air:
Her limbs' metallic sheen assumed
A place in natural order. Promenade
Des Anglais, where the tea-time sunlight falls,
The colour of a peach, on stone and stair.

Invisible exigencies, dynamic laws,
Invest the palm trees and the pink parquet,
Gods of the yellow Sports Bugatti,
Whose high, spoked wheels shone like the sun on sea.
In the loud car she took her leather throne,
As movement multiplied to incident.

The palm leaves hissed in that light breath of wind
Which trailed the man-made chiffon drapery,
Hung from her neck, into the blur of spokes.
Tensile strength and roar of wheel then did for her
What any rope or cord would do in time,
Without the strong, mechanic coil of this.

Most of the passers-by at once assumed
A stunt, perhaps a hoax: a girl illusorily strung
Before the plate-glass of the white hotels,
Garrotted by some pagan chariot wheel.
Even the locked drive and the sound of skid
Would rate a mere half-movement of the head.

3

Voices in the Next Room

Courtier's Speech

Who was the King?
The King was a man
Prone to turn turtle in a purple rage
And cleave the neck-bone
Of the nearest sycophant
With the nearest cleaver.

What of the King's mirth?
The King was his own jester. A wag
With a born flair
For the practical possibility
Of lobster-men boiled in their baths,
Or the trick board to spring them
To a spiked pit.
Not a dry eye in the whole house.

What were the King's lusts?
Rape was his aphrodisiac to murder.
As he rode by, the flames of our homes
Lit the skewered bellies of wives and daughters.
Our senile parents danced like whores
To win reprieve.
Being a married man himself,
He knew, when seeking information,
The true value of family relationships.

What was the manner of the King's death?
A whole peacock in his strangled belly.

And what after he died?
In his will he gave his gardens to the people
For their recreation.
We all agreed with his obituary.

'He was a man of more than life-size,
Of gruff repartee, extravagance.'
One couldn't help admiring, though, remembering
A monarch of the old school, whom
We shall not look upon again.

Musician's Speech

Keeping time in the King's time
In the boulevard cafés,
Wearing our disengagement like a rose:
Keeping time in the new time
In the old places
For those who saw the King's rope
Judder taut:
Accepted but not pictured
Returning collarless to children
And sheets that need changing
In rented rooms,
Holding opinions only in bed:

Critics remarked the absence of debate
In our public lives, not appreciating
That we, of all people,
Are not paid to make discords.

Scullion's Speech

The plot was one we all knew well,
This being real life—a simple story.
First the King would give a golden ring
To his faithful subject, the fisherman.
'Keep this ring and three years hence
Bring it again and share my kingdom,
Or lose it and die.'

Everyone knew this trick, even the hero,
Who pretended to be deceived, for the sake of art.
The ring was stolen, on the King's orders
And thrown in the river.
The hero pretended dismay and helpless search.
The day before he reported for death,
Two fish hung waggling in his net.
The plot required the gold ring
In the maw of the fish he ate for supper.

There was some surprise among the audience
When the little carcass proved empty.
Only the hero remained serene
With his neck stretched on the block
At the next dawn. A quiet smile,
Perhaps knowing the axe-blade was rubber.
Rubber or not, it severed him
From his confident twinkle.

It hardly seemed the place to clap or cheer.
His Majesty stooped and retrieved such gold
As could be shaken from the trunk's recesses.
And when he next went to his bedroom,
He found the widow, who was still quite young,
And her daughters, who were quite grown-up,
Inviting ambush, tongue in cheek.

The King's performance was voted best of all,
And this new version is the one most popular.
Myself, I was relieved when someone's lord
Belched and neighed loudly from the back:
We knew then it was all right to laugh.

Sorcerer's Speech

I, white magician, capped and robed,
Cast from my cloud the chant of peace:
That song's note enters like a blade
And halts the motion of the curtained heart.

Let but my hand command the sun,
And the blue world goes into black.

When windblown torchlight flaps
Like tapestry in shadow,
At my devising
Blood's joy shall sing a silent anthem
In the loins of bride and groom.

Who seeks the dead, shall find
In shadow-play my art makes all things new.

     ★

Let gold reward such harmless guile.
Tricks of my life's trade shall endure
When there are no more trades.

     ★

Often I see a coming time,
I watch the year, a crouching cat
Whose victim only sees it spring.
But first I bow, retire invincible.
I'm not the one who'd want to cut
Too near the royal nerve.
A certain reputation does for all.
So I dismiss the boy,
Set wig on block,
Pull off my own boots, sit alone
To nurse a foot's ache in a layman's hand.

Analogies

What is a heart?
A heart's an engine that stops once.

And what is 'once'?
That's first and last.

But if first is silver, like the morning,
And last is bronze, like the evening,
Then 'once' cannot be first and last.
Try again.

*

What is a heart?
A heart's a feeling that's with you always.

'Always' for me, or 'always' for always?
There is only one 'always'.

Which I am not part of.
Try harder.

*

What is a heart?
A heart is a habit you cannot break.

You cannot break ever?
Not once in a lifetime.

Yet mine has been broken in several places
And on various occasions.
Be careful.

★

What is a heart?
A heart is a limited system
One man can get into,
No man can get out of.

And you think that's a heart?
Then what would be love?
Clinically speaking, the question of love
Is not the heart's professional matter.

Letter to a Friend

Marie Corelli, Wendell Holmes, and Scott:
All sixpence on this shelf. The bent, black page
Of a photo album—nineteen twelve—
'The shooting party leaves The Hermitage.'

I saw your writing underneath the print
Of tweeds and gaiters, boys in grown-up caps,
And women dressed like frail, beribboned kites.
My quick hypotheses collapsed.

It was your writing, but you never knew
Scotland, the shooting, or The Hermitage,
Being too young then, and now being dead too long
To answer what the written words allege.

Under my hands and in bright, dusty air,
Coincidences fluttered, closed, and joined.
I turned the pages, still confronted
By the false identity these letters coined.

Upon the fly-leaf, in the same dead script,
A home address, two hundred miles from here:
From where you lived, not two. I closed the book,
Preferring not to have the whole thing clear.

Walking warm August streets, I pictured you
In usual static images, framed
Like that fading sepia world. Thoughts
Grudge you the voice and motion you demand.

But the ambience of a labyrinth
Walls up the bedlam of complete recall,
And between us the radiant distances
Fog like the spokes of a spun wheel.

Tannhäuser to Elizabeth

Our bodies meeting only through your eyes,
Our hands' negotiation must remain
That privilege you will not exercise.

Shades touch and fall. Now our twin shadow lies
A moment still. Breaths in closed rooms contain
Our bodies' meeting. Only through your eyes

The figures of shared thoughts politely rise
And turn to go. Their code does not explain
That privilege you will not exercise.

In me, love's cryptograms are otherwise:
Anger is ardour that has planned in vain
Our bodies' meeting only. Through your eyes

My breathless effort to devise
Coincidence of mind makes you disdain
That privilege. 'You will not exercise

Love's power and call it love,' your glance replies.
A curtain shimmers; clocks' hands move again:
Our bodies meeting only through your eyes
That privilege you will not exercise.

Lundy

For Paris Leary

'The island next passed into the ownership of
Bishop Heaven, at which time it was known as
"The Kingdom of Heaven" '—*Guidebook.*

Heaven's kingdom rises north of Hartland Quay,
Where Kingsley saw the inshore green
Turning to sapphire in the late Atlantic day.

Beyond the contours of the map's display
The island grows: through the long silences
Heaven's kingdom rises.

              North of Hartland Quay
The blind light stands, a tower in his sky,
Guarding a frame of mind. Dead sea-thoughts burn,
Turning to sapphire.

              In the late Atlantic day
The hollows walled by turf and cliff betray
No spirits of the place, but in their echoing rain
Heaven's kingdom rises north of Hartland Quay.
Mauve, flame-backed fish cruise among water flowers.
A tree
Twists over tawny water, like a dead witch leaning.
Turning to sapphire in the late Atlantic day,
Cut to glass fragments by the sun's quick play,
The ocean holds perspectives of the afternoon.

Heaven's kingdom rises north of Hartland Quay,
Turning to sapphire in the late Atlantic day.

Language Lesson

All this the master of the language knows:
Your conjugated errors cage you in
That you may learn at last what I say goes.

Decline 'I am.' Or so decline what follows
Is your own decline. Such word-play takes you in?
All this the master of the language knows.

Time's come for more complex inflections, those
To stretch your lip and nerve. You'd still begin
That you may learn? At last what I say goes

Beyond your least resistance? Truths repose
Out of your reach in this new tongue. I win
All this. The master of the language knows.

Shall purge you of, presumption. And you chose
'I am as good as you?' You won't decline
That. You may learn what I say? Goes.

The monologue too fast for crippled prose
To piece together in your own brains' din?
All this the master of your language knows,
That you may learn at last what I say goes.

4

A Guide to the Grounds

For Carol

Villa Buenaventura

Glazed mandarins on an inlaid vase
Link fingers under opulent sleeves:
Beneath tassel moustache and declining eyes
Smile their kings like thieves.

The white noon, like a basilisk,
Catches a stone flamingo's gaze;
Light's moving parallelogram
Depicts the lapse of days,

Whose late suns at our shoulders hang
Like brilliant evening parasols
And in pale, oblong monuments
Let shadows grace our walls.

Warm hours are the wood of a native tree
We fashion into souvenirs
To perplex the assured memory
In subsequent years.

Meanwhile, cool voices annotate
Thick sunlight, colour of a peach,
And exquisites with silken words
Parade the cadence of our speech.

Through mild evenings the equestriennes
Approach at an eloquent canter
Over elegant turf, till at the dwarf pines
The pledged hooves falter.

Their riders masked in proud device
Of inaccessible despair,
The pale arabian horses thud
Into the starlit air.

A Guide to the Grounds

Art being the paraphrase of nature.
    But, of course, you knew.
Below this belvedere, our willow-pattern bridge
    Jumps the whole ornamental view.
Stormy, unpolished sunlight on the lake
    Strikes like a chord between the trees;
Rain trills on water, as a hand
    That wakes Debussy from the keys.

With every footstep here I seem to trip
    On someone else's ancestors.
They say we have a ghost who never haunts
    But only sees and hears.
Late on a winter afternoon, the sun
    Lies yellow on that stable tower.
You see the minute hand from where we are
    But only hear the hour.

Then, on the open land, you are alone.
    You hear a single bird
Plain as a boatswain's whistle at that height
    Where all is overheard.
These formal gardens fill our afternoons,
    Being the only landscape we require.
Yet in such grace the graceless still contrive
    To walk the chronic tightrope of desire.

A madman built the house. Of course, you knew.
    Built it for love to haunt but no ghost walked.
Those patterned lawns beguiled his sanity,
    There, where we sat and talked:
His tragedy resolved in stone,
    Scrolled on Napoleonic urns,
Or by rain on the evening river
    In the slow pool's turns.

If once, on a winter day, his eyes might wake
   To be endowed with another man's estate,
His terrace, garden ponds,
   Carved lions at his gate,
A whole world waiting; would he see the change?
   The same mist pads the tree limbs, from the town
The same bell calls. The dead words flutter to the ground,
   While lake reflections catch the light and drown.

Fête Galante

Love in the park means putting on
The buckled shoe and velvet mask:
Respect for place makes it the least
That one should ask.
And a passing thought of the winter trees,
Their leafless nudity of gods,
Would make undressing out of doors
Aesthetically against the odds.

Under the lamplit, twilight boughs
The music calls its costumed slaves,
At whose soft heels the shadows run
Like open graves.
Slick trades of the mandolins
Bring Orpheus to the waiting ghost,
And Circe, the complete *madame*,
Plays hostess to the natural host.

Diana haunts the huntsmen's woods
In tights of gold *lamé*,
Breaks her shoe on a hidden root
But not a catch all day,
While in their shop-lit evening
The glad hermaphrodites
Pluck at their careful eyelids
Under drained, fluorescent lights.

Pump-Room Blues

A pastoral mist deploys from the black ponds
  By three o'clock. On level fields of vapour those
Square abbey outlines ride at anchor
  In tones of winter light that Ruysdael chose.
Pale aureoles of the tasselled lamps
  Fall short on the blind fog,
While on the hour the clock-trills call
  Thoughts' costumed ghosts to speak an epilogue.

Like arrow-heads, December birds
  Beat, black, over dwindling primrose skies.
Smoke dribbles from the pinewood bark,
  Sweet-perfumed as a wreath. Lone phrases fall,
Elude the lamplight's pools, and pass into the dark.

In bronze doré the putti hang,
  Fat boys caught up in golden trees,
Like flies racked on a web. They frame, below,
  A pier-glass which serenely forms
A room more ordered than the one they know.

Words fade to whispers round the plaster frieze,
  Mourning the hour's collapse. Soft questions find
No footprint in the level sand
  That skirts the desert island of the mind.

In the Wordsworth Bar

The flags, like the rhododendrons, are almost over;
The shrubbery gardens sombre as a wreath,
Where the turnstile, angel-like, shows out the lovers.
Here, like confetti, summer butterflies
Dance on the air we breathe.

The poet Wordsworth spent the night
Above the cocktail bar. The syphon sighs
Over each glass, discreet lament
Of lawful debaucheries.

'You ought to write—I think you ought—
I know you could—if I should say—
Loosely describing what I mean—
A rather neat *roman à clef*.'

The late and yellow sunbeams dance
Over the glass and moquetry,
Through liquid warm utopias
Of intellectual honesty.

'Yes. I would say I was as good.
Not better. No. But just as good
As any there. And, oh, I could
Describe such antics, if I would.'

One floor above, one century ago,
The old man dined. His life's two guests appear:
Facile rebellion and an easy cause,
Eating his art to a starvation here.
Sat at the sunlit ruin of the feast,
He yielded to a duty to be great,
Laboured to fill the pibroch with his wind
And howled lost grandeur at the years' locked gate.

'You have a kindly heart. You have
A journey over water, friends to greet,
Yet are not loved. Just here I see
The tall embattled stranger you shall meet.'

Birds loop across the sundialled lawns
Where, as the summer voices swell,
A slow anatomy of light
Embalms the Imperial Hotel.

Penny Telescope

The coin's drop lights a silent dream,
That smudged auras of the lens
May beguile their client of time and place,
While the past, like a *trompe l'œil*, takes him in.

Bands play in his other world,
Under a more reliable sky:
The unshuttered pageant at the tube's end
Welcomes back the refugee.

Green breakers curl in a pure glass
Over warm shingle, shimmer and hang:
The coloured segments of umbrellas move
Like a campaign.

Through leaves lie spandrels of light and water,
Where, like a martyr, lake azalea bleeds
Against late madder skies. On salmon-coloured mud
Rise the dark reeds.

Years later, the most immaculate passion
Declined to a calculated risk
And the scent of flowers was simple proof
Of a nose for decay.

Once the tasselled carriages
Bore the negotiators past:
Now the ultimatum of a coin
Expires at a shot.

The round stone of the image falls
Into its dark pool. The ripples die,
And starved remorse, like a thin cat, slinks
Back to penumbras of its walled city.

Inigo Richards

a Prospect of Halswell House

Out of its usual element, in yellow light
Of sun on sand, the warm façade
Swims backwards from the picture frame.

Pillars depend over the flat design
From hidden wires that thread the view
With flying ballet of perspective art,

Its choreographer the moving eye.

Caught within lily ponds of tarnished gold,
The orange, ornamental fish,
Like segments of a fruit, hang in the murk

Of an eternal jelly. Then warm rain
Through jasmine or mimosa in the dusk
Of August seen in March evokes no scent

Beyond the floor-wax of the exhibition-room.

Inigo's sun is a reflecting sphere,
His earth the port of senses for the dead:
His weather over Halswell is our mood.

Like yellowed newspaper, this painted sky
Awaits the lover of absolute landscapes,
Whose prompting, unfulfilled, shall make him prey
Of every labyrinth of absences.

Death and the Maiden

(From Clovis Trouille)

Wax mannequin:
A smooth parade of shoulder, hip, and calf,
Whose length of neck and leg
Elate the elegant giraffe,
While beauty, mute in an underworld,
Is her own cenotaph.

Black spears of the cypress trees
Lance her pale night:
Rain rattles the broken stone
By a wrenched, iron gate,
And the sky's flash hits the wet, ribbed span
Of a bat's-wing flight.

Pale satin flanks, black-stockinged legs
Should grace her catafalque.
Their necromantic image
Wakes dead gestures and provokes
Thoughts of a velvet privacy
In death's hermetic dark.

Through grilled and gothic arteries
Her masked voluptuaries prowl,
Bloom on their moonlit offerings,
Dead as wax fruit in a bowl.
Yet love, like a mutual leprosy,
Robs their five senses still.

Her images, like jungle cats,
Roam sleep's pathetic fallacies:
Flames in their serpent brackets
Light a black, enclosing sky,
And presences of air admire
The apple of a long-dead eye.

Villanelle

The summer clichés of a song
Disturb bleached sand and dazzling air:
Time's dream is not where we belong.

In flashing parody, the long
Scythe harvests gorse and prickly pear.
The summer clichés of a song

Throb through the hot day. In the strong
Sky, glittering silences repair
Time's dream. Is not where we belong

This shimmering edge of waves, along
These landscaped distances that blare
The summer? Clichés of a song

Are real: voices through pines, among
Warm cones like lush grenades, declare
Time's dream is not. Where we belong,

The golden playthings of the throng
Echo in their genteel despair
The summer clichés of a song:
Time's dream is not where we belong.

Twilight at the Zoo

Leaves hiss in a dark surge
Under the apricot flesh of cloud:
Over cropped lawns the conifers shift
Through their dark, elegant latitudes.

In a blue night zoo
The tame cats hunch
In a spelt language of attitudes.

A wreath of black sky tightens
Round incandescent cumulus,
Deepening an open theatre
Through shadowed terracotta urns.

Apes cry in their carillons of love,
While in the stride of the trapped cat
The crossing night winds hover.

The arched goat treads blossoms that fall
In pink drifts on the concrete hill,
Calling the sleek dogs' conical snouts
To their lupine prowl through orchards of steel.

5
Memoirs

For Laurence and Menna

We strive with none, for strife is impolite
In any world where each must play his part.
Crossword and anagram enrich our minds.
Nature we geld, and after Nature, Art.

                                        T.H.M.

Memoirs

I

Unaware that the light was bad; that the band
Had begun; that the shrubs, pink and crimson,
Thickened the warm salt wind; that the dark girls,
As they strolled, stared most of all at him,
Though without curiosity: but aware
That his passing would be marked by no feast
Of baked meats nor by funeral games,
He sought in the present no omen of his past.

Yet reading the whirlpool's purling tornado of water,
Turning the scansion that mulled island air like honey,
Their rhythms insisted he once stood there
At the tall prow of a swan's-neck galley.

Now on his evening sea, an effete violet,
A pale sun tapers like rippled copper
Under clouds of gunpowder grey. Once, though,
He heard Troy's walls go down like a crowd's roar.

Dark seas were wine-dark then.
No gentle crown would fit such killers' heads,
Not even Priam's, withered tight on bone,
Life passing at a tremor.
Though not Odysseus, he had known the same;
Had seen the muscle-warp upon the back
Of drowned sailors. A prince's flawless eyes
Watched the world's morning, mapped by the tall ship's tack.

Now, by his borrowed canvas chair,
Waves of wet slate glimmer like carapace,
While, at the first high firework, bursts
'Orchestral Gems from Massenet'.

✳

'You ought to find yourself a girl,' they said.
They said, 'Your old Achilles knew a whore
Is more use in the long run than a goddess,
Or the yellowed lustre of a ten year's war.'

'You seem to have no pastimes, as we do:
Pictures or gardens, coins or reading heads,
Leisure, adultery in moderation.
All work and no play,' they said.

2

Then through the twilight, while the long arcades
Chimed with their coffee cups, was time for him
To haunt the public gardens, statuary
Beyond the yellow tulip heads. Cast in dove-grey
The dead past apes itself, under the trim,
Flowered urns along the colonnades.

After the music, back to the tall house
With the moon pale as the face of a girl
In a pool of bright water.
His tread lets loose the sprung sighing of boards,
Worn mats, packed stiff with dust, curl
At their corners. Night hours recount his loss.

First from these walls fell the golden armour,
Leaving only the household gods and a smell
Of mice. Next, the private heroes, out of vogue
As a uniformed sepia snapshot
Set in the fragment of an aircraft's wing, fell,
And left only their pale, discoloured oblongs there.

After the honoured dead were voted quaint,
Love and the face of love eluded him.
Frail as moon's double in night's black water,
Her touch like a spider thread across his face,

Her dream pale as a wafer of translucent bone.
Once he would match her blood's warmth with his own,
Now like an airborne web her thought recurs,
Cold as the practice of an antique grace.

On fringes of the stagnant pools of lamplight,
Shadows squeak and chatter, pretending to be ghosts
To see him run. But in the tawny glare
He casts no shade. Beyond his reach
The vacant mirrors gibber at their host,
Who flaunts no image, now or any night.

★

They said, 'The last one here used to have girls
All hours of night. And underneath the bed,
After we'd turned him out, were bottles.
And he scratched at our doors,' they said.

They said, 'It's plain to see *you* are a gentleman,
Your reverential face, white cloud of hair.
You treat us right, you'll like it here,
Once you do as we say,' they said.

3
An amber pool of Russian tea, plucking at light,
Quivers along the wall of grey smoked glass.
On autumn carpets, Aubusson designed,
Late afternoons of music pass.
'Life at its best assumes sonata forms,
A, B, and A again.' His metaphysics pace
The patterns of the carpet. This, the last time
To say the right thing: here, the available space.

The past recedes to where Caruso sings
Or Paderewski's bright technique recalls
Not Chopin on Majorca in the rain
But hours in 1920s concert halls.

Yet once on a grey June morning, while in town,
He had watched Elgar crossing Wigmore Street.
Had seen the patriotic music halls,
Was born where history and legend meet.

As for the rest, the Abbé Liszt
Walking the gardens of the Tivoli,
Or Chopin's cortège, to the *marche funèbre*,
Leaving the Place Vendôme—these were mythology.

All gods require a relic, and the past
Lived in his senses only,
Its present shrine a replica
And image of his face, pale on a glass of tea.

★

They said, 'Old men must come to understand
What's what: which side their bread is buttered, if at all.
We do not outlaw any art of life,
But we know what we like,' they said.

'What counts is being part of here and now,
Seeing all points of view, not choosing one.
And if you want to be a hero—fine:
But in your spare time,' they said.

4

Aware that all flowers in a garden have their names,
But never knowing what the true names are,
The acid scents of wet April earth
Smelt to him like a dead star.
Disdaining the gift of scrutiny,
He pondered the rain-sky's passing flush
Of salmon light through saffron cloud
Under an empyrean of pale ash.

The old meanings melted, long dispossessed,
Where the Chinese lanterns dripped on wet palm leaves,
Leaving only untenanted thoughts to rise
With a garden pagoda's stilted poise.

Knowing time is the one truth not to be bribed
To release locked beauty, or to disclose
Which fruit must ripen, he grew content
With elegance and, when that failed, with silence
Or an ode on some coming into fashion.
Then the heroes mingled with the promenaders
Until the heroes became the promenaders,
And, when he looked for them again, had gone for ever.

Teacups and rhymes, with their gentle intrusion,
Chimed life away as he slept again,
In the pall of stagnant light, and the hot
Metal smell, the prelude to thunder rain.
He dozed where the musty sweetness of roses
Hangs, thick as dust, in a king's orchard,
Where the fruit of his dream-flower would instantly rot,
Like the husks of burnt pages, if touched.

6

Noirs

The Ancestor

'Own up! Own up!' Carruthers senior cried,
'I want the name of each boy in this House
Who's having filthy thoughts! Own up at once!'
The small change rang, his ravaged face assumed
Tints of the Empire on the class-room globe,
Lips glistened, wet as in his infancy.

'Which of you dreams of stripping kitchen-maids
Instead of following through the bowler's arm?
Who draws the gardener's daughter in his mind,
Lewdly uncovered from her waist to knees?
Own up!' he begged, 'My patience has run out. . . .'

'Which of you is it?' Carruthers senior screamed,
'A mind fit for the bog-house wall!'
(The syntax crumbling under passion's force.)
'No one gets tea until a boy owns up!
Until he does, I won't eat tea myself!'

Three blushed, and Samways, G., began to cry.
Carruthers senior raised him by the hair,
Clear of his desk, and dropped him to the floor,
Then kicked him as he lay there.
'Moss! Dyer! Fetch the boxing gloves!'
And Samways cringed, his nose now tingling
At the coming blows. 'No, sir, not me!
I don't like girls,' he sobbed.
'Boys, eh?' Carruthers senior rasped, 'The worse for you!
I won't have filthy homos in my House.
Now, fight me, Samways! Fight me, boy, I said!'

For twenty years Carruthers senior ruled
The roost in Mayflower House.
He took weak-bladdered, bronchial boys

And built them into men.
The boy who wet his bed
Ran twenty-five times round the rugger pitch.
The boy who coughed in prayers
Got castor oil for fourteen days.
And even those who afterwards
Would never speak his name again,
Returned as boys (each night they dreamed)
To where Carruthers senior sat
And waited for the culprits to own up.

Once, when the summer holidays began,
Carruthers senior in a fit of gloom,
(Eight empty weeks still echoing ahead,
Bereft of owning up and punishment)
Went to the sports room for the high-jump rope.
Little Carruthers, coming in at seven years old,
Looked up and saw the feet, and further up
His father's smiling face. A silent face
But grinning fit to bust.

On Founder's Day a dwindling group returned
And stood in silence for the man
Who made them men.
They knew the difference now, the place
Run by some lad who never raised his voice
But taught by kindness, mutual respect.
They meditated on the changing world,
Almost colliding with a happy boy
Who ran towards the undergrowth,
A freshly-heated knife-blade in his hand.

A Sense of Outrage

What Paula said to Deirdre was,
'And then there's you-know-what in bed.
You'd think they'd have a man to share
That load.' Deirdre stopped counting in her head,
Coughed and said, 'Sixty-nine,' aloud.
(A mutual stare; a squittering
Of smothered laughter.)

In his unsprung chair Mr Templar lies.
Pondering Rosalind's Ganymede thighs
And envying hairy Miss Linnett,
Whom once he drew approaching Rosalind,
Wearing a *gaude mihi* made of glass.
(The men and married women laughed.)

Templar one evening, just for fun,
Had wired their place for sound.
Next day we watched the slow tape turn,
Anticipated limbs and hems askew,
Imagined groans and cataclysmic cries.
There was a single kiss, but not before
Rosalind's 'Will you hear my prayers, please, Mum?'
And, 'Now I lay me down to sleep',
And, 'That's a good girl', as the light went off,
And Templar's 'Quite enough, I think!'
And a deep sense of outrage.

That winter, after Rosalind caught cold
And died (leaving poor Deirdre to take games),
The worst thing happened.
An indecent wreath, there at the graveside,
For the world to see.

'From Mumsie to her little girl. Sweet thoughts.'
As Templar rightly said,
'If she had worn black pants in mourning,
One could understand.'
But this thing made us shiver.

So Miss Linnett no longer shaved,
And lasted just one term,
Then left to join an order of Poor Clares.
(Enlisted, rather.)
As Paula said,
'We all know what *that* means!'
And, although no one did,
Each of us nodded, just to be
Entirely on the safe side.
Wouldn't you?

From an Observer's Notebook

What fascinated us was how
Their spirits rose when each new cask was broached,
Though every breath of water in their throats
Brought closer still their final thirst.
Those who observed their sleep recorded
That it lay on them like snow, marked by the print
Of wolf pad through the black trees' path.

By day the sun turned their sky white
But each new cask would bring them close,
Made friends of those two who had fought
For the last pulped grape on the sand path
After the programmed death of the vine.
We observed willing exchanges of dreams, like sweets,
Memories of walled gardens, chimes and sundials,
Where girls in brittle lacquer buzzed like golden insects.

The level fell and fell. Loose ends
In the nerves' complex caught.
Each fly that settled touched them like a pin.
The girl who bore a still-born child
Would feed her lover with her milk.
(The project-leader recollects
Cases of this in Continental wars.)
When the glands ran dry
Her own thirst made it kind
To end her quickly, and quite neatly too.

(The cadences of grief revealed
New campanologies of love.)
You can believe, by this time, no one had
To ask for volunteers to man the screens.
Yet, right until the last cask had run dry,

They vetted each of us quite strictly.
Some people would have saved the last one,
But what you do for one should go for all.
Others enjoy this sort of thing too much.
You can't afford to have the wrong type here.